Micronesians on the Move
Eastward and Upward Bound

About the Series

Pacific Islands Policy examines critical issues, problems, and opportunities that are relevant to the Pacific Islands region. The series is intended to influence the policy process, affect how people understand a range of contemporary Pacific issues, and help shape solutions. A central aim of Pacific Islands Policy is to encourage scholarly analysis of economic, political, social, and cultural concerns in a manner that will advance common understanding of current challenges and policy responses. The series editors and members of the editorial board are all affiliated with or on the staff of the Pacific Islands Development Program (PIDP) at the East-West Center.

Pacific Islands Policy

ISSUE 9

Micronesians on the Move
Eastward and Upward Bound

FRANCIS X. HEZEL, SJ

EAST-WEST CENTER
COLLABORATION, EXPERTISE & LEADERSHIP

THE EAST-WEST CENTER promotes better relations and understanding among the people and nations of the United States, Asia, and the Pacific through cooperative study, research, and dialogue. Established by the US Congress in 1960, the Center serves as a resource for information and analysis on critical issues of common concern, bringing people together to exchange views, build expertise, and develop policy options.

THE PACIFIC ISLANDS DEVELOPMENT PROGRAM (PIDP) was established in 1980 as the research and training arm for the Pacific Islands Conference of Leaders—a forum through which heads of government **PIDP** Pacific Islands Development Program discuss critical policy issues with a wide range of interested countries, donors, nongovernmental organizations, and private sector representatives. PIDP activities are designed to assist Pacific Island leaders in advancing their collective efforts to achieve and sustain equitable social and economic development. As a regional organization working across the Pacific, the PIDP supports five major activity areas: Secretariat of the Pacific Islands Conference of Leaders, Policy Research, Education and Training, Secretariat of the United States/Pacific Island Nations Joint Commercial Commission, and Pacific Islands Report (pireport.org). In support of the East-West Center's mission to help build a peaceful and prosperous Asia Pacific community, the PIDP serves as a catalyst for development and a link between the Pacific Islands and the United States and other countries.

Published by the East-West Center

A PDF file and information about this publication can be found on the East-West Center website. To obtain print copies, please contact

Publication Sales Office
East-West Center
1601 East-West Road
Honolulu, Hawai'i 96848-1601 USA

Tel: 808.944.7145
Fax: 808.944.7376
EWCBooks@EastWestCenter.org
EastWestCenter.org/PacificIslandsPolicy

ISSN 1933-1223 (print) and 1933-172X (electronic)
ISBN 978-0-86638-231-1 (print) and 978-0-86638-232-8 (electronic)

Table of Contents

Executive Summary

Is out-migration an admission of a Pacific Island nation's failure to fulfill its economic promise and provide the jobs that its citizens seek in a modernized society? Or is it a legitimate alternative strategy for development, through the export of surplus labor, in lieu of the more conventional methods recommended by donor nations and international financial institutions? In this paper, Francis X. Hezel, SJ, reviews the 30-year history of migration from one Pacific Island nation, the Federated States of Micronesia (FSM), and examines the current status of its migrants with an eye to shedding light on this question.

Although the first traces of migration from the FSM were apparent in 1980, Hezel reports, the outflow increased sharply with the implementation of the Compact of Free Association in 1986. In return for exclusive strategic access by the United States, the Compact granted FSM citizens entry into the United States and its territories to establish residence and work. This report traces the growth of the early migrant communities on Guam and Saipan, and the ensuing migration eastward to Hawai'i and the US mainland.

The size of the outflow from the FSM has grown with the years, even as the island economy has sputtered. At present, fully one-third of all FSM-born people live outside their island nation. Hezel presents the results of an important—first-of-its-kind—2012 survey of FSM migrants, showing that an ever-greater share of the migrant population is settling in the continental United States. From 1995 to 2000, the survey data show, the net gain of FSM citizens in the continental United States was 700 annually; during the next 12 years, that number grew to 1,200 annually. In North America, FSM citizens are able to find more abundant jobs, reduce their cost of living, and escape some of the negative stereotypes found on Guam and in Hawai'i. The survey revealed that the median hourly wage for Micronesian migrants in the US mainland was about $11 an hour—much higher than the wage in Hawai'i and on Guam.

In this report, Hezel is concerned with more than merely numbers. He also lays out some of the difficulties migrants from the FSM faced in settling into their new homes and tracks the changes in their living conditions over time. Even if Micronesians continue migrating at their current pace, there is clear evidence that their living conditions are improving with time. So too are their potential contributions to American society and to their families and friends back home.

Micronesians on the Move
Eastward and Upward Bound

Introduction

Emigration as a Pacific-Wide Phenomenon

Emigration is a common phenomenon throughout much of the Pacific, but until recently it has been a badly misunderstood one. Labeled as *brain drain*, emigration was for a long time generally considered a threat to island nations, inasmuch as it was thought to deprive them of those educated people who might work the economic miracles needed to make their countries self-reliant. The departure of these people, or even less-educated islanders, to other countries was thought to be a net loss for the islands they were leaving.

Yet, in the case of the Federated States of Micronesia (FSM), like the Republic of the Marshall Islands and the Republic of Palau, emigration was deliberately provided for in the negotiations with the US government that led to the Compact of Free Association. Far from being viewed as a regrettable occurrence, emigration was seen as a necessary provision to permit the drain-off of excess population—which at the time the Compact was signed was still growing at a rate of well over 3 percent annually—and a safety valve in the event that the nation should fail to meet its economic development goals. As demographer Michael Levin and I put it in our 1990 article on Micronesian migration, "Future emigration, then, far from being seen as a menace that threatens to deplete the islands' human resources, is counted upon as an essential element in the Micronesian states' strategy for economic and political survival" (Hezel and Levin 1990, 42).

> Emigration was seen as a necessary provision to permit the drain-off of excess population.

In the late 1980s, at the cusp of the much-heralded globalization breakthrough, the world was beginning to reassess the large-scale shift of workers from one country to another that had been occurring for years. Whether it was called export of labor or a shift of supply to meet demand elsewhere, migration could be legitimized as a sound economic strategy, not necessarily seen as an admission of failure. Remittances sent home by laborers working abroad were making a significant contribution to the economic health of many nations around the globe. It was not just Mexico and the Philippines that benefitted from remittances, but Pacific Island states like Tonga, Samoa, and the Cook Islands (Connell and Brown 2005). Who was to say that the same benefits from emigration could not be enjoyed by the FSM and the other freely associated states?

Micronesian Migration

Migration from the FSM, long a subject of speculation, is now an undeniable reality. Thanks to the provision in the FSM Compact of Free Association allowing free access to the United States, one out of every three FSM citizens now lives abroad. About 50,000 FSM people and their children currently live in the United States or one of its jurisdictions, in Guam, or on the Northern Mariana Islands, while the resident population of the FSM numbered 102,000 in the 2010 census (FSM 2010).

The FSM national government, understandably, wished to obtain factual data that could provide a clear picture of the extent of migration and the social conditions of those Micronesians* living abroad. Hence, Levin and I were contracted by the FSM government to conduct a survey of the migrant population in the United States and its jurisdic-

One out of every three FSM citizens now lives abroad.

tions. The final survey report, presented to the government in August 2012, offers the most detailed view yet of the migrant communities in several different locations (Hezel and Levin 2012). The report examines the social and economic status of these communities, comparing them with one another and with the FSM itself, while exploring the ways in which these migrants continue to maintain ties with their home islands. I will be drawing heavily upon the survey report for the portrait of the FSM migrant community today in the last section of this issue of Pacific Islands Policy.

In the first part of this report I will offer a history of the growth of migration, especially in the years since the Compact took effect in 1986. The concern is not simply to track the expansion of numbers or migrants in each of the major destinations, but to observe the changes that have occurred in the

*In this report, *Micronesians* refers to people from the Federated States of Micronesia.

living conditions of migrants and even in the way they come to be perceived by their host communities. An understanding of the development of the migrant communities is indispensable if we are to grasp how they function the way they do today.

History of Migration in Micronesia

Beginnings

Palau was the first island group in Micronesia to experience heavy emigration, with a total migrant population numbering several thousand by 1980, well before the rest of the area began to show any similar movement. Emigration from Palau began early—soon after World War II. The preferred destination was Guam, where, by 1953, there were already about a hundred Palauans residing on the island. For the next two decades emigration from Palau to Guam and other destinations was measured at 50 or 60 people a year. After 1972, however, as young Micronesians began attending college abroad in higher numbers, Palauan emigration increased sharply to about 240 a year[1] (Hezel and Levin 1990, 46).

Emigration from other parts of Micronesia at the time remained minimal. The 1980 US Census recorded the number of Micronesians living in the United States, apart from full-time college or high school students, as no more than a few hundred. According to an early article on the subject, "The US Census figures suggest a total FSM emigration (whether short-term or permanent) of approximately 600–900 nonstudents, 100 Trukese, 200 Pohnpeians, no more than 50 Kosraeans, and 250–550 Yapese" (Hezel and Levin 1990, 58). Among these earliest migrants, significantly enough, was a sizeable cohort from the low-lying outer islands of Yap—people who had left their home islands while young in search of an education, but who recognized the difficulty of finding suitable employment either in their own subsistence economy or in the district capital of Yap. They and the handful of others who had drifted away from Micronesia during the 1970s were the harbingers of what was to come.

Meanwhile, Micronesia had just experienced an education explosion that was having an enormous impact on the islands (Hezel 1979). During the 1960s (actually, 1962 to 1972), the rapid education buildup on the elementary and secondary level throughout the Trust Territory resulted in the opening of new schools, the hiring of American contract teachers, and the expansion of the high school enrollment everywhere. The number of students enrolled in high school throughout Micronesia soared. From fewer than 50 a year in

1960, the number of high school graduates in what would later become the FSM exploded to 360 yearly by the end of that decade, and then continued to expand until it reached 800 a year by 1979 (Hezel and Levin 1990, table 6). Beginning in 1972, when Micronesians were first declared eligible for Pell Grants for college, an increasing number of islanders went overseas to get a college education. Those Micronesians who attended college abroad in 1970 numbered no more than 200 or so, while by 1978 the number would explode to 2,400 (Hezel and Levin 1990). The educational expansion, considered long overdue by many, exposed many hundreds of young Micronesians to the United States for a few years. Although not all of those who went abroad to study graduated from college, they all returned to their home islands with the expectation of a salaried job.

Educational expansion, considered long overdue by many, exposed hundreds of young Micronesians to the United States for a few years.

During the late 1970s and early 1980s, the extension of US federal program funds to the area and the sizeable increase in government positions as the former Trust Territory was reorganized into separate political entities offered nearly enough new jobs to provide for the returning college students. Thanks to the rapid expansion of the governments throughout this period, an unemployment crisis was averted among those who expected that their degrees would by the key to a public-sector job. Between 1980 and 1995, the number of jobs in the FSM increased from 10,000 to nearly 16,000, a rate of growth that was nearly as high as during the high-growth 20 years that preceded this period (see figure 1). For a time, at least, the economy—founded as it was on an expanding government sector—was able to keep pace with the expectations of the young who had benefited from the education explosion of the 1970s. But that was bound to change.

Early Post-Compact Migration (1986–1988)

In November 1986, the Compact of Free Association between the United States and the FSM was finally implemented. The Compact, which granted Micronesians free entry into the United States to "lawfully engage in occupations and establish residence as non-immigrants in the US and its territories," offered islanders the opportunity for legal emigration for the first time (FSM 1982; Title I, art. 4). The provision was anticipated as essential to the survival of a small-island nation with a high population-growth rate but limited resources and a dubious pathway toward economic development. Even so, the rapidity with which this option was exercised surprised many.

Figure 1. **Employment in the Federated States of Micronesia, 1960–2010**

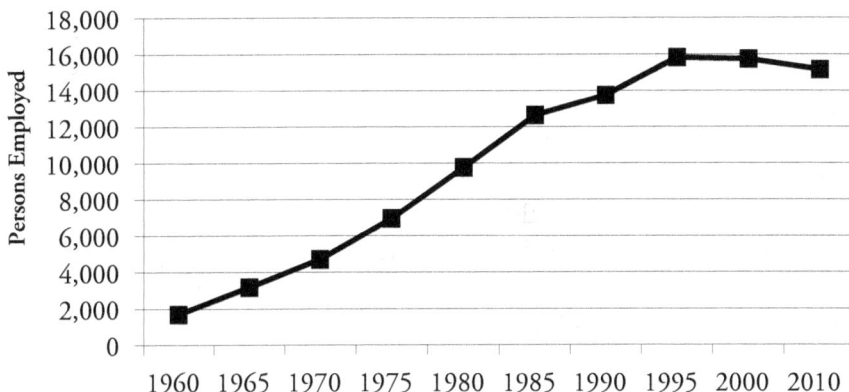

Sources: US Department of State, Trust Territory annual reports; Asian Development Bank EMPAT annual economic reports for the FSM; and 2010 FSM Census.

In 1980, according to the Guam Census, there were 410 FSM residents on Guam, half of whom were students residing on the island temporarily (US Census Bureau 1980, table 26). The size of what might be called the migrant FSM community on Guam, residents who were not college students, was no larger than 250. By 1988, just two years after the Compact had gone into effect, a sample survey indicated that the FSM resident population on the island had grown to about 1,700, nearly two-thirds of whom were Chuukese. The projected number of residents in this sample was consistent with the estimate derived from a Guam Labor Department survey (Hezel and McGrath 1989). Chuuk, with a migration rate much higher than that of other states, offered a glimpse of the type of people moving to Guam at that time. An informal survey taken in Chuuk showed that many of the migrants were relatively uneducated and were seeking menial jobs in the hotel industry or fast-food places around the island (Hezel and McGrath 1989). This was a pattern that would continue in the years to come.

Guam's economy, by good fortune, was booming at just this time. The tourist industry, spurred by the devaluation of the US dollar and the strength of the yen, began its climb to new heights as Japanese travelers arrived in unprecedented numbers from 1984 on. This in turn stimulated a construction boom and a rapid growth in private business. Private-sector employment on the island doubled between 1983 and 1988, creating over 15,000 new jobs during those years (Hezel and McGrath 1989, table 4). Guam's labor supply, however, was very limited. With an unemployment rate of only 4.5 percent, the island would have been hard-pressed to provide a workforce large enough to handle all the new jobs that were being created. Moreover, Guam was subject to severe restrictions on importing foreign labor; H-2 work permits for aliens were limited and had to be individually approved by the governor. The appearance of Micronesians seeking work on the island afforded a providential labor supply that the island badly needed at the time.

Even as Micronesians were flocking to Guam for jobs, they also continued to move to the Commonwealth of the Northern Mariana Islands (CNMI). There they found jobs in the large Asian-run garment factories that were just then opening to take advantage of exemptions on import taxes to the United States and in the small businesses that were sprouting up as the local tourist industry expanded. Even before implementation of the Compact in 1986, Micronesians trickled into Saipan to take up residence there because there were no restrictions on entry inasmuch as the Northern Marianas had once been part of the Trust Territory. The estimated flow came to "perhaps 300 a year to the CNMI in the period 1983–1986" (Hezel and McGrath 1989, 61).

Overall, then, an estimated 3,100 FSM citizens had migrated north by 1988, including "a resident FSM population in the Northern Marianas of 1,400 and a movement of 1,700 FSM citizens to Guam" (Hezel and McGrath 1989, 61). Not only did the expanding economies of both places offer jobs, but their proximity to the FSM allowed emigrants to maintain close contact with home and to visit relatives there from time to time. The early migration was described in one article:

> There is a great deal of shuttling back and forth, as would only be expected of a people whose ties with family and birthplace remain as strong as Micronesians' are. This circular flow resembles that of Samoans between their islands and the western US except that much smaller distances in the Micronesian circuit encourage more frequent visits home (Hezel and McGrath 1989, 61).

Developing Migration to Guam and the Northern Marianas

Migration rates northward continued to grow even after the initial surge. On Guam, the flow from the FSM had been about 600 or 700 migrants a year during the first two years of the Compact, a rate that continued until 1990. The

Table 1. **Micronesian Migrant Population: Guam, CNMI, and Hawai'i**

Year	Guam	CNMI	Hawai'i
1980	410 Guam Census 1980 (a)	552 CNMI Census 1980 (i)	
1988	ca. 1,700 Household survey by Thomas B. McGrath (b)	ca. 1,400 Estimate based on number of school- children (b)	ca. 405 Estimate from US Census 1990 (m)
1990	2,944 Guam Census 1990 (c)	1,817 CNMI Census 1990 (i)	951 US Census 1990 (m)
1992	4,954 University of Guam Micronesian census (d)		
1993		2,261 CNMI survey of migrants (j)	
1995		1,961 CNMI Census 1995 (i)	
1997	5,789 Levin, survey of migrants (e)		3,786 Levin, survey of migrants (n)
1998		2,199 Levin, survey of migrants (k)	
2000	8,573 Guam Census 2000 (f)		
2003	9,098 Levin, survey of Guam migrants (g)	3,097 Levin, survey of migrants (k)	5,091 Levin, survey of migrants (o)
2008	16,358 US Census Bureau statistical survey (h)	ca. 1,560 Estimate based on US Census Bureau survey (l)	ca. 8,320 Estimate based on US Census Bureau survey (l)
2012	13,558 Hezel and Levin, 2012 survey of FSM migrants (p)	4,286 Hezel and Levin, 2012 survey of FSM migrants (p)	7,948 Hezel and Levin, 2012 survey of FSM migrants (p)

Sources: (a) US Census Bureau 1980, table 26; (b) Hezel and McGrath 1989; (c) US Census Bureau 1990; (d) Rubinstein and Levin 1992, Rubinstein 1993; (e) Levin 1998, table 2; (f) GovGuam 2004, 30; (g) Levin 2003, table 3-3; (h) US Census Bureau 2009; (i) CNMI 2000, table 2; (j) Levin 1998, 3; (k) Levin 2003, table 3-11; (l) US GAO 2011, 63; (m) Levin 2003, table 15-4; (n) Levin 1998, table 1; (o) Levin 2003, table 3-4; (p) Hezel and Levin 2012.

outflow increased to about 1,000 a year between 1990 and 1992, as the Guam economy flourished, and by 1992 the migrant population on Guam numbered just short of 5,000 (see table 1). In late 1992, however, Guam's economy experienced a sudden downturn because of several serious typhoons and a slump in tourism brought on by the Japanese recession. Migration from the FSM to the island waned for the next few years, although the number of FSM citizens crept up to 5,789 by 1997 (see table 1). In the meantime, other destinations had opened up for potential Micronesian migrants.

The Northern Marianas, especially the main island of Saipan, had always been a fallback option for FSM migrants. Just as early migrants had moved there before the implementation of the Compact allowed them free entry into Guam, so they again drifted into the Northern Marianas between 1988 and 1993 at the rate of fewer than 200 a year (see table 1). But the appeal of this destination was limited. Even after Guam seemed no longer able to absorb new workers after the slump in 1992, the inflow of FSM migrants to the CNMI was never very heavy. The migrant population there appears to have grown by about 100 a year from 1993 to the present.

During the first six years of the Compact period (1986–1992), the average annual migrant outflow to Guam and the CNMI was about a thousand persons, the equivalent of 1 percent of the Micronesian resident population. The emigration northward, especially to Guam, would continue through the remainder of the 1990s and the following decade at a reduced net rate of 500 persons a year. Throughout the ups and downs of Guam's economic fortunes, then, FSM migration to the island remained strong, even if many of these migrants would eventually move on to other destinations.

The relative ease of travel between the FSM and its neighbors to the north allowed migrants to visit their home islands frequently. Some of the migrant laborers maintained such close social bonds with their families and communities that they were virtually commuters (Rubinstein and Levin 1992, 351). Those who left for Guam or Saipan had the freedom to return home permanently if personal circumstances demanded, with little or no rupture of kinship ties. Indeed, many of the Chuukese who moved to Saipan in these early years did just that, as the return migration figures show (Hezel and Levin 1996, table 4).

Even as the FSM population in Guam and the Northern Marianas was growing, it was also becoming more settled. In the Northern Marianas, between 1990 and 1993, the 15–29 age cohort dropped from 44 percent to 34 percent, the percentage of children rose sharply from 20 to 30 percent, and the over-60 age bracket showed a slight increase. At the same time, the dependency ratio nearly doubled, rising from 33 to 62, indicating an increase in the number of nonworkers and suggesting that the migrant household in the Northern Marianas was beginning to resemble that in the migrants' home islands (Hezel and Levin 1996). The migrants' housing, too, was reminiscent of what they would have had back home—large, sprawling buildings without some of the conveniences that the migrants in Guam might have enjoyed, but with plenty of room for family and friends.

Much the same kind of change was going on in Guam, even if it wasn't immediately evident. The early surveys of the migrant populations and the analyses by Donald Rubinstein, an anthropologist at the University of Guam, and others provide us with a body of literature describing the evolution of these migrant communities.[2] These studies remain as relevant today as when they were written because they lay out the dynamics of change in a migrant Micronesian population. The pattern they describe can shed as much light on what is happening today in the mainland United States as it did on Guam and in the CNMI 20 years ago.

These dynamics are summarized in an article I coauthored with Levin (Hezel and Levin 1996, 98–99):

> The earliest FSM migrants to Guam were predominately young males in search of jobs. Many of the original households were inherently unstable, composed as they were of several young men in their 20s or 30s working at low-paying jobs and pooling their income to cover rent and other expenses (Hezel and McGrath 1989, 58–60). In the absence of a viable authority structure and generational depth, such "peer-group households," as Rubinstein terms them, were continually "dissolving and reforming, with new arrivals moving in, others moving out" (Rubinstein 1993, 260). Rubinstein went on to note the gradual evolution of this fragile type of household into more typically Micronesian forms. In the second stage of the pattern Rubinstein identified on Guam, two-generation households emerged around a nuclear family, but they contained a potpourri of loosely related kin and friends. In the final stages, the members of the household were selected according to the kinship principles normative back home, and grandparents or other older people were added, giving the household important generational depth (Rubinstein 1993, 260–261).

All this meant that the new migrants of this period represented something much more than additional bodies crowded into small housing units. These new migrants included older people, many of whom spoke little English and so were unemployable, but who would provide childcare and stabilize the households (Hezel and Levin 1996, tables 11 and 13). The "young and the wild" of the first generation of migrants were being tamed as they took spouses, had children, and summoned older members of their families to join them. As the migrant households became multigenerational, an authority system like the one they had known back home was soon established. The consequences were double faceted. The recklessness stemming from weekend drinking may have diminished, but those additional migrants filling out the households temporarily expanded the welfare lists of those receiving government benefits. While this was happening, of course, pressure from the government of Guam intensified, as it sought federal assistance as compensation for these expenses. Soon the US Department of the Interior developed guidelines to help Guam and other affected areas submit their appeals for Compact-impact help from the US government (US GAO 2011, 31).

The Other Side of Migration on Guam

Government officials on Guam had been voicing concern over the impact and cost of Micronesian migrants from the outset. But a report on the 1992 Census of Micronesians on Guam concluded that "so far the Micronesians are probably more of a boon than burden for the Guam economy, because of their contribution to the labor force and their tax payments to the Guam treasury" (Rubinstein 1993, cited in GovGuam 1996, 24). The author of the report added, "As a community, Micronesians who pay taxes pay a higher proportional tax because of their low ratio of nonworking dependents to workers." Even as their households were filling out, Micronesians were forced to retain a high employment rate if they hoped to support those who were living with them. Because of the low salaries that most FSM migrants received for their entry-level jobs, anyone capable of holding down a job was expected to look for work to supplement the family income. Hence, the employment rate for migrants somehow continued to rise in good economic times and in bad: the rate of migrant employment increased from 34 percent to 39 percent between 1988 and 1994, even as the number of jobs held by FSM migrants expanded from 577 to 2,509 (GovGuam 1996, 25).

The migrants, of course, incurred a double financial burden. Not only did they have to provide for their household members in their new home, but they retained obligations to their family and friends back on their home islands as well. The 1994 FSM Census provided the first measure of remit-tances from the migrant communities abroad. According to census data, nearly 15 percent of all households in the FSM reported receiving remittances, with the income from remittances totaling $1,260,000 (FSM 1994, table 18). This figure, which could well have been underreported, was a sign that the tide had changed and that the money flow was running into the FSM rather than in the other direction. These remittances were just the beginning of what would become a significant source of income for the FSM in years to come.

Still, the governments of Guam and the CNMI had legitimate concerns over the sudden arrival of their new guests. A 1993 survey of Guam residents' reaction to the influx reported a strong consensus that Compact migrants, most of them FSM citizens, had made a major impact on Guam since the implementation of the Compact six years earlier (Smith 1993).[3] The areas most heavily affected, according to the re-spondents, were housing, education, and health care. In addition, mention was made of an issue that is bound to come to the fore in any area experiencing heavy immigration: the difficulty of integrating very different cul-tures into the way of life of the host country. "This unexpected influx caught Guam unprepared for the resulting population boom," the survey concluded (Smith 1993, 23).

> The governments of Guam and the CNMI had legitimate concerns over the sudden arrival of their new guests.

The most widespread and strongly voiced criticism was that Guam should have been allowed more control over immigration to the island—something that then and now lies in the hands of the US government. Many wanted to set up screening procedures for prospective immigrants, as was done with Asians, to ensure that the migrants had prospective work. Their fear that unemployed immigrants would become a burden on Guam's social system was not unfounded, as events showed. Yet, the terms of the Compact of Free Association plainly afforded access to the United States and its territories for any FSM citizen who wished to live and work there. US legal provisions, made without consultation with Guam, seemingly had considerable finan-cial and social impacts on the island. This point of contention between the US government and Guam, which would later be echoed in Hawai'i, was the basis for Compact-impact claims against the US government. The claims would be grounded in the enabling legislation that accompanied the US Con-gress's approval of the Compact. After disavowing any intention to do harm to any entity, the enabling legislation says, "Congress hereby declares that, if any adverse consequences to United States territories, commonwealths, or the State of Hawai'i result from the implementation of this Compact of Free Association, the Congress will act sympathetically and expeditiously to redress those adverse consequences" (cited in Levin 1998, 1).

Finding an affordable place to live was one of the main challenges the migrants faced on Guam. In the Guam Migration Report for 1993 (Coulter 1993, v), the housing shortage among FSM people was described as acute. Compact migrants, who represented only 4 percent of the Guam population, made up 28 percent of the 1,800 families on the waiting list for GHURA (Guam Housing and Urban Renewal Authority) assistance and 24 percent of the 100 families on the Guam Rental Corporation list. Meanwhile, homelessness was all too common among Compact migrants. Many of them found assistance in shelters for the homeless: 76 percent of the clients at Guma San Francisco, 52 percent of the clients at Guma San Jose I, and 64 percent of the people at Guma San Jose II were Compact migrants. It appears that at least 1,235 of nearly 5,000 migrants,

> **At least 1,235 of nearly 5,000 migrants, or about 25 percent, were homeless in 1992 for at least part of the year.**

or about 25 percent, were homeless in 1992 for at least part of the year. The homeless rate among Micronesian migrants appears to have greatly fallen in subsequent years, but the newcomers remained heavily dependent on subsidized low-cost housing. By 1995 nearly 15 percent of all subsidized housing on the island was occupied by Compact migrants (GovGuam 1996, 86).

Education of the migrant children was not as pressing a problem for the migrants or for the government. The influx of many new schoolchildren of different ethnic backgrounds was a situation the Guam Public School System had faced before with the earlier waves of Filipino and Korean students. In 1992, 1,242 Micronesian immigrant children were in the school system—the equivalent of the total enrollment of two average-size schools (Coulter 1993, vii). Two years later the number had risen to 1,447, but the worst of the rapid expansion was over (GovGuam 1996, 26).

The high crime rate among migrants was another issue raised in the early years. In 1992, FSM citizens were reportedly involved in 13.5 percent of all arrests, although they represented only 4 percent of the total population of Guam. The arrests, however, were mainly for minor offenses, especially drunken and disorderly conduct, assault, and DUI (Coulter 1993, 107). Since the migrants accounted for only 4.7 percent of the total inmate days in prison—a number roughly proportionate to their share of the general population—we can assume that most of the arrests were on relatively minor charges that did not usually result in jail time (Coulter 1993, 111). The same general pattern held true at the end of the decade, according to a report on crime statistics among Micronesian migrants. In 2000, FSM migrants, who made up about 6 percent of the general population on Guam, accounted for about 15 percent of all arrests, but only 4 percent of all those in prison (GovGuam 2000).

When Guam's economy slumped in the mid-1990s, even as the number of migrants was increasing, public reaction toward the newcomers took a more negative turn. Even migrants from islands with strong ethnic and historic links to Guam began to be viewed as competitors for the social services that were now operating under tight budgetary constraints. In 1990, the government of Guam paid only $265,000 in welfare to Compact migrants, most of them FSM citizens. By 1994 it was spending nearly $3 million, or 16 percent of its welfare budget, to take care of the migrants (GovGuam 1996, table 35). Part of the reaction to what long-time residents of Guam were beginning to see as competition for limited benefits was a bill introduced into the Guam Legislature cutting the welfare benefits offered to "non-citizens and non-alien residents" of Guam.[4] The new migration into Guam had turned into a pitched battle for funding, one in which Guam and the US government were pitted against each other, with the new migrants positioned precariously between the opposing forces.

Continuing Migration to Guam and the Northern Marianas

Despite the drop in homelessness, FSM migrants on Guam clearly remained financially hard-pressed. As the migrant population on Guam doubled between 1990 and 1997, the number of households increased by only 38 percent, suggesting that people were being packed more tightly into housing units than ever before. Moreover, the median income for the migrant household had dropped from $27,581 in 1990 to $22,119 in 1997. If these figures had been adjusted for inflation, the drop would have been even more striking (Levin 1998, table 12). The picture that emerged from this 1997 survey was of a community in which more of its members were forced to seek jobs that were as low paying as they had been in the past. More people were being asked to work longer hours in order to meet the rising cost of living on Guam.

Much the same was true of the FSM migrants living in the Northern Marianas. Between 1990 and 1995, as the size of the average household increased, the median household income fell from $18,503 to $17,043 (again unadjusted for inflation) (Levin 1998, table 18).

But if the migrants faced financial straits on Guam and in the Northern Marianas, the future back home was certainly no brighter for anyone who sought wage labor. By 1995, as the FSM prepared for the start of the final five-year funding cycle of the first 15-year Compact, the nation was bracing itself for the drop in US funding that would accompany it. With a 20 percent cutback in US funds ahead and national credit overextended, the FSM had to submit to a series of reforms led by the Asian Development Bank that would trim the number of government jobs throughout the nation. Since government had always been the bedrock of the island economy, the entire economy began to shrink. In 1995, for the first time in over 40 years, there was no significant increase in the number of jobs (see figure 1). Nor would there be any significant increase in the years ahead. With no new jobs to attract them at home, more Micronesians than ever began to seek their futures abroad.

Hawai'i, the Alternate Destination

We may safely assume that some FSM citizens began drifting into Hawai'i even before the Compact took effect in 1986. Just a year later a reported 405 FSM citizens were residing there, and by 1990 the number had grown to just under a thousand (Levin 2003, table 15.4). Hawai'i was relatively close to FSM, even if not quite as accessible as Guam or the Northern Marianas. Moreover, Hawai'i had been one of the "college towns" to which growing numbers of young Micronesians had been coming for years. The University of Hawai'i at its Manoa and Hilo campuses, Hawai'i Pacific University, and Chaminade College (now Chaminade University) had been the schools of choice for many Micronesians since the late 1960s. It was inevitable, then, that Hawai'i would sooner or later become a destination for FSM migrants.

Some of those Micronesians who had attended school in Hawai'i stayed on, often living with relatives who had established a home there years before. Before long a nucleus of FSM residents was formed, allowing further migration to occur with greater ease and increased speed. In a pattern that can be observed worldwide, those who had already settled into the community would offer newcomers shelter and a reassuring sense of familiarity in their new home, along with guidance in adjusting to the culture and tips on where they might find work. This pattern would be repeated time and again in more distant communities as FSM migrants began to settle in the mainland soon afterward.

The first full census of Micronesians in Hawai'i, conducted in 1997 by Michael Levin, counted 3,786 FSM citizens (Levin 1998). The next census, in 2003, showed 5,091 FSM people (Levin 2003). By 2012 the number of FSM migrants living in the state had grown to 7,948, according to the most recent survey. Since 1997, therefore, migration to Hawai'i, as to Guam, has been accelerating, despite the many attractive possibilities offered to migrants in the US mainland. The number of migrants to Hawai'i, which had grown by a little more than 200 a year between 1997 and 2003, increased by over 300 a year between 2003 and 2012.

One of the reasons for this accelerated migration to Hawai'i was the quality of health services offered there. Micronesians who required dialysis for kidney problems brought on by diabetes, or who needed chemotherapy for cancer, could find treatment that was unavailable to them back home. Many individuals with less-serious health issues could also obtain the medical assistance they needed in Hawai'i; sometimes they made repeated visits if their condition demanded it. The relative ease with which people could get back and forth to Hawai'i made it an ideal treatment center for people with health problems, or even a retirement home for those with chronic health needs.

> The relative ease with which people could get back and forth to Hawai'i made it an ideal treatment center for people with health problems.

The 1997 census of FSM migrants in Hawai'i presented a snapshot of the early Micronesian community that was very different from that of the FSM migrant communities on Guam and in the Northern Marianas. For one thing, the average household size in Hawai'i (3.5 persons) was much smaller than on Guam (6.4) and in the CNMI (5.1) (Levin 1998, 23–24). The stringent laws limiting the number of occupants in most low-cost housing units were a check on the island tendency to welcome all newcomers to share living space in the flats of earlier migrants. In any case, less than half (45 percent) of the FSM migrants surveyed at the time saw themselves as remaining in Hawai'i permanently. This was in sharp contrast with people from the Marshall Islands, 75 percent of whom declared that they were there to get a job and settle down (Levin 1998, 24). This early generation of FSM migrants seemed to look upon Hawai'i as more of a way station to somewhere else. For some, it might be a stopover before their return home, especially after medical problems were treated; for others, it could be a stepping stone to a more affordable and permanent home in the US mainland.

Yet the number of migrants from Micronesia continued to grow in the late 1990s and through the following decade. Most took jobs in drugstores, fast-food outlets, and gas stations as they struggled to make ends meet. Others were recruited for low-paying jobs on plantations, like the young men brought from Pohnpei and Chuuk to work in the pineapple fields of Maui. Soon there were a number of small businesses staffed almost entirely by Micronesians. One person from Chuuk who began work at a car wash was promoted to supervisor within a few years, and soon afterward nearly the entire staff was Chuukese.

Some Japanese teppanyaki restaurants were staffed almost entirely by Pinge-lapese migrants. A few of the more enterprising and better-educated migrants found managerial positions, a handful took professional positions as doctors or lawyers, and one founded a multimillion dollar IT business that is well known throughout the state (Hezel and Samuel 2006).

Nearly everyone faced the problem of affordable housing; the cost of hous-ing in Hawai'i can be prohibitive for those earning little more than minimum wage. New arrivals might normally move in with relatives for a time, but before long would usually find themselves a burden to their families. Overcrowded apartments would bring complaints from the landlords or resident managers, often forcing the new arrivals to leave for other quarters before their hosts were evicted. Some packed themselves into a single apartment and pooled their earnings to pay for the rent. Yet, this was usually no more than a temporary solution because of the fear of eviction for overcrowding. One common re-sponse to the problem was described in an issue of *Micronesian Counselor* that focused on migrants:

> Most islanders right off the plane can find a relative with whom to live,
> but soon they find themselves becoming a burden to their family. They
> may find a minimum wage job, but they soon learn that they can not
> support themselves this way, nor do they qualify for government services
> with a job and a permanent address. With pressures mounting between
> themselves and their relatives, many new migrants simply move out,
> declare themselves indigent, and throw themselves on the mercy of the
> government (Hezel and Samuel 2006, 4).

Many of the migrants did just that. By 2000, 14 percent of all FSM mi-grant households were on welfare, according to the US Census (Levin 2003, 150). Homelessness among Micronesian migrants, a growing problem during these years, drew public attention when a series of Honolulu newspaper ar-ticles publicized the disproportionate share of the state's homeless services uti-lized by Micronesians.[5] In a study titled *The Not-So-Silent Epidemic*, Michael Ullman (2007) pointed out that the number of Micronesian migrants (from the FSM and the Marshalls) relying on homeless shelters had tripled between 2001 and 2006. By 2006, Micronesians made up more than 20 percent of the shelter population, even though they accounted for only 1 percent of Hawai'i's population (Brekke, Filibert, and Hammond 2008; 33).

During a visit to Honolulu in 2006 to film a video, the Micronesian Seminar staff found abundant evidence of homelessness:

We found that a good many Micronesians are on welfare and quite a few have declared themselves homeless, partly because being listed as homeless gives people a leg up on finding affordable housing in a state where even the smallest unit is prohibitively expensive at market prices. We visited two homeless shelters—one for men and the other for women and families—and found a number of Micronesians in each. We even saw a few Micronesians hanging around Ala Moana Park with their possessions in plastic bags. We passed an island family packed into a van, children asleep in the back seat and the trunk piled high with bags of all sorts—what seemed to be the family's household goods. We could only conclude that this family was living out of its van. One Marshallese woman sitting at a park bench with a very large plastic bag beside her told us that she had been staying with her relatives for a while, but left them when the place became very crowded (Hezel and Samuel 2006, 3).

It was for good reason that the majority of FSM migrants to Hawai'i envisioned themselves as transients. Despite the high cost of living, salaries were poor for anyone taking the kind of entry-level job that most migrants held. In 1997, the median household income for migrants was only $11,437, and 35 percent of those who had moved to Hawai'i since the Compact went into effect in 1986 were living below the poverty level (Levin 1998, 26). Public assistance in the form of welfare payments and access to shelters for the homeless remained a problem for years, one well-advertised in the Hawai'i press. Still, the little data we have for those years show an improvement in the condition of the migrants. Per capita income for FSM residents of Hawai'i, for instance, was recorded at $6,279 in 2003, representing an increase of nearly 50 percent over the $4,213 figure for 1997 (Levin 2003, table 3-16). The median income for households showed an even sharper increase during this six-year period, nearly doubling to $22,390 by 2003 (Levin 2003, 52).

As the FSM migrants became more settled in, their lives in Hawai'i took on many of the features of home. Even their churches were soon headed by island pastors, as Protestant ministers who had moved to Hawai'i presided at local language services for migrant congregations. Catholic deacons, especially from Chuuk, also provided spiritual care for their people. The churches offered a center for the social life of migrants, as well as a real, but still underutilized, contact point with the FSM migrant population in the state.

On to the US Mainland

People from different parts of Micronesia were moving to the mainland United States even during the early years of the Compact, but their numbers remained relatively few. Marshallese had begun moving into a few communities such as Costa Mesa, California, since the early 1990s. Palauans, of course, had already begun drifting to the US mainland decades earlier, but in small numbers and without concentrating in any single place. FSM migration to the mainland, on the other hand, only caught the public eye in the late 1990s as recruiters began to show up in the islands and enlist dozens of people at a time to fill work slots in the mainland. In 1999, about 200 women were brought to the United States to be trained to work in health-care facilities for the elderly. About that same time Pohnpeians were recruited to work in the theme parks of Central Florida, especially SeaWorld and Walt Disney World in Orlando.

Business prospects were still bright in the United States during the late 1990s as the economy continued to expand. Cheap labor was a valuable commodity. Recruiters, popularly known as "headhunters," roamed the world looking for sources of inexpensive labor. With no visa problems to complicate entry into the United States, Micronesia was an attractive source of menial labor. For FSM citizens,

For FSM citizens, the US mainland appeared an attractive option to Guam, the Northern Marianas, and Hawai'i.

who were still hard-pressed to find work in an economy that had been virtually stagnant since 1995, the US mainland appeared an attractive option to Guam, the Northern Marianas, and Hawai'i. Guam and the Northern Marianas were looking ahead to retraction in their economies, even if entry-level jobs could still be found in both places. Guam especially appeared to have reached a saturation point for migrants: housing was still difficult to find, welfare benefits were no longer dispensed as liberally as before, and public reaction was strong against what appeared to be unlimited migration from the islands to the south. Hawai'i, too, offered serious challenges for FSM migrants—among them, the high cost of living and the difficulty of finding affordable housing.

Micronesians had already established a number of beachheads in the US mainland, thanks in great part to the heavy inflow of young students attending college during the late 1970s and 1980s. Once again, college towns, with their small settlements of Micronesians, became magnets for further migrants. Kansas City, Missouri, home of Park University and Rockhurst University, has attracted such a steady stream of students from the FSM that it has become one of the two largest settlements of Micronesians in the mainland; currently, Kansas City is home to two or three thousand FSM migrants. Portland, Oregon, with a Catholic university that once attracted hundreds of Micronesian students, is now the center of a sprawling island population comparable in size to that of Kansas City. Even Corsicana, Texas, site of Navarro College, once a favorite college choice for Yapese, now hosts a good-sized community of Yapese and Chuukese outer islanders. William Carey University, a small evangelical college with an international enrollment, has been another of those magnets, attracting about a hundred Micronesians to the Pasadena, California, area.

Yet, problems arose for some of the migrants to the US mainland. Not all Micronesians recruited during the late 1990s were happy with their work. Headhunters had made extravagant promises of free plane tickets to the United States, educational opportunities abroad, and other benefits that were unmet. Workers were sometimes dismayed to find that unexpected deductions from their paychecks left them with sums well below the US minimum standard wage. One Micronesian displayed a check stub showing that his take-home pay for a two-week period amounted to $3.14 an hour (Levin 2003, 149). The plight of islanders exploited by certain recruiting agencies caused a sensation when two reporters, Walter Roche and Willoughby Marianao, exposed the abuses in a series of press articles.

> A yearlong investigation by the [Baltimore] Sun and the Orlando Sentinel has found that Muller and DeMichele are key players in a ruthless international business in which thousands of Pacific islanders are shipped to the United States on one-way tickets and consigned by "body brokers" to one to two years of virtual servitude at nursing homes and amusement parks. The workers are bound by contracts that require them to pay damages of up to $6,250—equivalent to as much as half their annual wages—if they walk off the job (Roche and Willoughby 2002).

Nonetheless, many did walk off the job, often finding other positions in other mainland cities. Relatively few returned to their home islands, where opportunities were too limited to offer any real hope of employment. Whatever the problems they faced in the United States, most decided to make their future there.

Many of the Micronesian women who were recruited to engage in training programs in basic nursing so that they might serve as attendants in the nursing homes did the same. Those who were dissatisfied with their working conditions left for other towns where they might hope for better employment. In time, they spread to a number of small communities throughout the mainland such as Park Falls, Wisconsin, where they took jobs in other nursing facilities.

The women working in such places brought in their male relatives, husbands and others in their family, as they built up modest-sized communities in their adopted homes. The men took whatever positions they could find in lumberyards, mills, and manufacturing plants in the area.

If the adjustment problems faced by FSM migrants in the mainland have been similar to those in Guam, so were the strategies employed to cope with these problems. Multigenerational families have been formed in the US mainland—as they do wherever migrants settle—even if some households showed no sign of this during their initial years in their new homes. The family, in turn, would depend on the pooled money-earning efforts of several of its members, as shown by the one-to-one dependency ratio of the families sampled.[6]

Likewise, the migrant community assumed many of the features of an island village, as the Micronesian Seminar video team observed in 2006:

> Everywhere we went, we found that Micronesian immigrants were quick to establish networks that bound families together. These networks were often church-based, usually Protestant rather than Catholic, and offered opportunities for common worship, sports and recreation, and strengthening of their sense of cultural identity. The networks served as a means of support for island families even as they afforded a measure of social control over the behavior of individuals in the network. Individuals who wished to slip off and go their own way could certainly do so, but at their own risk. The networks were an undeniably positive force in the communities we visited (Hezel and Samuel 2006, 10).

Regular gatherings of the typical migrant community to celebrate birthdays or other special events were common throughout the mainland United States. In some places, the communities would host annual games for other migrants in the surrounding area, sometimes drawing others from hundreds of miles away. Nearly always there was a recognized authority figure in the small community, a "chief" whose status is as often achieved as ascribed, who would be responsible for reminding newcomers of the behavior that is expected of them during their stay. In many respects, then, the migrant community in the mainland was a partial replica of a village community back home.

In many respects the migrant community in the US mainland was a partial replica of a village community back home.

Growth of the FSM migrant population in the US mainland has been rapid in recent years. Although no census of this population has ever been taken, we

Table 2. **Distribution of FSM Migrant Population, 1995–2012**

Year	Guam	CNMI	Hawai'i	US Mainland	Total
1995	ca. 5,000	1,961	ca. 2,000	ca. 3,000	12,000
1997	5,789	2,199	3,786	ca. 4,200	16,000
2000	8,573	ca. 2,500	ca. 4,400	ca. 6,500	22,000
2003	9,098	3,097	5,091	ca. 12,700	30,000
2008	16,358	ca. 1,560	ca. 8,320	ca. 15,800	42,000
2012	13,558	4,286	7,948	24,048	49,840

Note: 1995–2008 figures for Guam, the CNMI, and Hawai'i derived from surveys conducted by Michael Levin; 2012 figures derived from the survey by Hezel and Levin. Total calculated on the basis of "missing population" for the FSM. US figures represent the difference between the estimated yearly total of FSM migrants and those accounted for in other destinations.

can calculate the approximate number based on the "missing" FSM population, presumed to have migrated, less the total of the migrant community on Guam and in the Northern Marianas and Hawai'i. According to this computation, the FSM population in the mainland would have numbered about 3,000 in 1995 and 4,200 in 1997. The migrant population would have climbed to 12,700 by 2003 and 24,000 by 2012 (see table 2).

Micronesian Migrants: How They Fare Today

About the Survey
The data used in this section came from the survey of Micronesian migrants that Michael Levin and I conducted in 2012 at the request of the FSM national government. Levin, an anthropologist by training and a demographer by trade, has worked on several previous censuses of Micronesian migrants in Hawai'i, Guam, and the CNMI. The 2012 survey used here differs from past ones in two important ways. First, its scope was to survey a representative sample of the migrant population rather than to do a full enumeration, as past censuses attempted to do. Second, this survey included the FSM migrant

community in the US mainland for the first time. Hence, the survey sacrifices depth of onsite interviews for geographical comprehensiveness.

In addition to the household interview data gathered by enumerators, the survey team also met with focus groups of select migrants in each site. We also gathered background information and data from government offices on homelessness, crime, and other adjustment problems. Finally, the team had at its disposal the reports and data tables from earlier surveys of migrant populations conducted between 1992 and 2003.[7]

The 2012 survey placed the total number of FSM migrants at 49,840. In the absence of accurate gate-count figures for the net outflow from the FSM, the survey team had to rely on the "missing population" for the FSM. The difference between what the population would have been, with the natural growth rate factored in, and the actual resident population constitutes the number of those who have presumably left for other places.[8]

This section will draw on this survey to offer a brief profile of the migrant population in each of the four destinations. The profile will present trends in the size of migration in recent years, general characteristics of the average household, economic status of the migrants, and other indicators of the well-being of the migrant community. The section concludes with a summary of the major findings in the survey that highlights the differences between migrant communities in the four destinations.

Guam

The total Micronesian migrant population on Guam at the time of the survey was calculated at 13,558. This figure, I should note, is much smaller than the estimate of 24,737 FSM citizens on the island projected in the most recent Guam Compact-impact report[9] (GovGuam 2011, 36). Chuukese individuals account for 78 percent of the migrants on Guam. Their overrepresentation in the FSM migrant population on Guam can be explained by the proximity of Guam to Chuuk and the ties that have been built up during the 1990s. The breakdown of the migrant population for other states is: Pohnpei, 14 percent; Yap, 4 percent; and Kosrae, 2 percent.

Between 2003 and 2012, the net increase in the FSM population on Guam appears to have been about 500 each year. The 2012 survey data indicate that five years previously a total of 1,872 were living somewhere other than on Guam (Hezel and Levin 2012, table G09). Hence, the number of those migrating to Guam from other places was recorded at 374 a year over the period 2007–2012. Most of these, 310 yearly, came directly from FSM, but another 60 a year moved to Guam from the United States and its territories, particularly the CNMI due to the crash of its economy. An additional 1,776 children, or 355 each year, were born to FSM migrants on Guam during this recent five-year period (Hezel and Levin 2012, table G07).

According to the data in the survey tables, then, the FSM population would have grown by 729 yearly, with roughly half of that increase coming from direct migration and the other half by on-island births. But this apparent yearly increase of 729 fails to take into account those who have died or left the island. The difference here—between the 729 total added to the population each year and the 500 net yearly increase—suggests that Guam is still serving as a way station for people who move on to Hawai'i and the US mainland afterward.

> An additional 1,776 children were born to FSM migrants on Guam during this recent five-year period.

Slightly more than 40 percent of the FSM migrants on Guam in 2012 were US citizens (Hezel and Levin 2012, table G04). The great majority of these, 96 percent, were people born on Guam to Micronesian parents. They represent a class that is entitled to certain government benefits by virtue of citizenship, so it is significant that their number is growing rapidly.

The median age of the migrant community on Guam, according to the recent survey, was 20.5 (Hezel and Levin 2012, table G01). It has dropped from 23.1 in 1988 and is now even lower than the median age of the population in the FSM (21.3).[10] This drop occurred as the original migrants began to raise families and have their own children. The size of the average migrant household on Guam in 2012 was 5.4 persons, with rather little variation between ethnic groups. The number of persons in a single unit has dropped over the years—from 7.3 in 1992 to 6.7 in 1997, 5.8 in 2003, and 5.4 in 2012.[11] This drop in household size over the years may be a sign that Micronesian migrants on Guam are acculturating, or perhaps they are simply yielding to the insistent pressure against overcrowding.

According to the 2012 survey, 39 percent of all Guam migrants aged 15 and over, worked for cash the previous week (Hezel and Levin 2012, table G15). Many of these people found entry-level jobs working in convenience stores, fast-food places, and hotels. They took jobs mainly as housemaids, security guards, clerks, busboys, and gardeners, although a few assumed higher-paying positions such as teachers, office managers, and guidance counselors. Two even worked as college professors. The average salary for the FSM migrant was $19,765 yearly, but half of all employees earned no more than $14,000 (Hezel and Levin 2012, table G17). Indeed, 60 percent of the FSM workforce on Guam made less than $8 an hour (Hezel and Levin 2012, table G15) at a time when the minimum wage was $7.25 an hour.

Of the 2,512 households on Guam, 2,307 had some cash income during the past year. (Presumably the other "households" included the homeless, students living in the dormitories, or even small families entirely dependent on others for their support.) For those households with some income, the average household income was $24,832, but half of these households were living off no more than $18,000 a year (Hezel and Levin 2012, table G18). The typical household (with 5.4 members) needed nearly two earners (1.8 is the average) to generate even this modest level of income. To put it another way, the average cash earner was supporting with his pay two other people in the household.

Homelessness, as we have seen, has been a problem for FSM people on Guam from the very beginning. As early as 1992, 25 percent of the nearly 5,000 migrants on Guam were living in shelters for at least part of that year (Coulter 1993, v). The problem has continued up to the present. In 2007, shelters for the homeless were reportedly accommodating 267 FSM migrants, who comprised 25 percent of the entire shelter population on Guam. By 2012 the problem had become even more acute—the number of homeless people from the FSM had grown to 646, and these individuals now made up 58 percent of the shelter population.[12] The problem has been a persistent one for migrants and the numbers today are shockingly high, but the figures should be put in perspective. Although the FSM share of total homeless shelter space is nearly as high as it was in 1992, it is worth noting that shelter space on Guam has not expanded significantly since that time. Furthermore, the 646 homeless in 2012 represented just 5 percent of the total migrant population, a striking decrease from the 25 percent homeless rate among FSM people in 1992.

One lingering concern about the Micronesian migrant community on Guam has been the individuals' reported penchant for getting in trouble with the law. Although the survey data did not include information on this topic, the information officer at the Department of Corrections reported that 141 FSM people were then in jail out of a total prison population of about 550–600. Hence, FSM migrants, who represented 8.5 percent of the total Guam population, made up roughly 25 percent of the total prison population. Their crimes are usually drinking and driving, assault, and family violence, and their sentences tend to be short. Most do not have the money to post bail so they may spend more time in jail than people of other ethnic groups. Among those convicted of more serious crimes, four or five adults from the

FSM have been judged guilty of sexual abuse and are serving sentences of 15 years or longer.

Over the years, as we have seen, arrests of FSM migrants have been disproportionately higher than their share of the population. In 2010, for example, Micronesians, who represented 8.5 percent of the population, accounted for 63 percent of all the arrests reported on Guam for that year.[13] That figure was surprisingly high. For most years during the past decade, the FSM share of the total arrests ranged between 25 percent and 35 percent.[14] The number of arrests of Micronesians may have been three or four times greater than their percentage of the island's population, but the migrants generally did not spend as disproportionate an amount of time in prison. In 2000, for example, when Micronesian migrants made up about 6 percent of the general population on Guam, they accounted for 15 percent of all arrests, but only 4 percent of the prison population (GovGuam 2000).

Northern Mariana Islands

There were 4,286 Micronesians in the Northern Mariana Islands, according to the 2012 survey.

The breakdown of the FSM population by state reflected rather closely the resident population in the FSM itself. Chuukese, numbering 2,656, made up 62 percent of the total. Pohnpeians, at 1,055, came to 25 percent, while the 434 Yapese comprised 10 percent. Kosraeans, the smallest group at 141, amounted to only 3 percent of the total (Hezel and Levin 2012, table C03).

The median age of the FSM migrant community in the Northern Marianas was 19.4, lower than that of the FSM resident population or any of the FSM migrant communities elsewhere. The low age in the CNMI, as on Guam, suggests that the FSM migrants have been settled into their new homes long enough to have young children.

The other data in this survey, too, indicate that the FSM community in the Northern Marianas is a long-established one. A good majority—57 percent—of the Micronesians living in the CNMI had US citizenship, compared with the 39 percent holding FSM citizenship (Hezel and Levin 2012, table C04). This can be explained by the fact that 53 percent of the Micronesians residing in the CNMI were born there and so automatically were eligible for US citizenship. Nearly half of the remainder arrived in the CNMI in 1994 or earlier, so they have been in the island group nearly two decades or longer (Hezel and Levin 2012, table C05). The rest, about one-fourth of the present residents, migrated to the CNMI between 1995 and 2012, with a uniform distribution of migrants throughout that period averaging 53 a year.

Migration from the FSM to the Northern Marianas has been episodic, as table 1, which traces the growth of migrant population, shows. During the late 1980s through 1993, there was a spurt of heavy migration to the CNMI. Again, from 1998 to 2003, the FSM population showed a larger than normal expansion. Otherwise, growth in the FSM migrant population has been slow. Since 2003, the date of the last census, the FSM population has expanded from 3,097 to 4,286. The growth of 1,200 during a nine-year period yields an annual expansion of about 130, but the survey data reveal that close to 60 percent of this was through on-island births rather than migration.

There were 838 Micronesian households in a total migrant population of 4,286, so the average household contained 5.1 persons. The average yearly income for all 822 households with some cash earnings was $25,451, a figure reflecting the salaries of government employees and others on the high end of the employment scale. Half of these households, however, had yearly earnings of less than $11,000 a year (Hezel and Levin 2012, table C17).

There are no homeless shelters on Saipan or on any of the other islands in the Northern Marianas, and homelessness does not seem to be a real problem in the CNMI. We were told by informants that two young men from the FSM are without a permanent residence on Saipan; supposedly, they left their families and chose to live on the street because of drinking or drugs.

Homelessness does not seem to be a real problem in the CNMI.

None of the survey data reflected criminal activities among Micronesians in the Northern Marianas. Although we visited the CNMI Department of Public Safety, we were not able to obtain data on arrests, convictions, or imprisonment of migrants. From interviews with individuals and the focus-group discussion, we concluded that FSM people were not perceived to be lawbreakers or stigmatized as a deviant minority group.

Hawai'i

The total Micronesian population in Hawai'i was 7,948, according to data collected in the survey. As a segment of the population, FSM people are nearly invisible, representing as they do less than 1 percent of the state population of nearly 1.4 million. Yet this migrant group, which shares the bottom rung of the social ladder with Marshallese, has caught the public eye because of the disproportionate claims it is said to be making on social services.

The median age of the migrants was 26.9, much higher than the 21.3 median age recorded for the FSM in its 2010 census (FSM 2010, table B1). This indicates that the migrant population in Hawai'i is more recent and less settled than in some other places, notably Guam and the CNMI. Kosraeans, show-ing a median age of just 18.9, were the exception. Half the Kosraean residents in Hawaiʻi were children of the head of the household. The 2012 survey data suggest that Hawaiʻi has been one of the principal destinations for people of that island from the outset. Just as Guam served as the migration fallback for Chuukese, so Hawaiʻi has done the same for Kosraeans.

A significant number of Micronesians (703), said they moved to Hawaiʻi principally for medical reasons (Hezel and Levin 2012, table H04). This is ten times the number of those on Guam who reported health concerns as the reason for their move. Yet, there is another attraction of Hawaiʻi which, despite the high cost of living, probably weighed heavily in choosing it as a destination. Living in Hawaiʻi means living on an island, with all that that means: the food, the weather, the feel of the place, the culture, and the close-ness to home. For this reason, we might conclude that there is and always will be a sizable group of migrants who do not want to go any farther than Hawaiʻi.

Of the more than 8,000 Micronesian migrants in Hawaiʻi, the survey data tell us that 1,056 arrived in the state sometime before the end of the 1990s (Hezel and Levin 2012, table H05). Hence, only about 100 a year arrived dur-ing the period 1988–1999. The figures go on to show that about 300 a year arrived between 2000 and 2004, and about 450 a year came from 2005 up to the point of the survey. All of this confirms that migration to Hawaiʻi has ac-celerated greatly in more recent years.

The survey data show that of the 2,253 FSM people who had moved to Hawaiʻi in the past five years, one-third had moved from Guam, the CNMI, or the US mainland. The remainder had presumably come from the FSM during that time. This would mean an immigration rate of nearly 300 people a year arriving from the FSM during the period 2007–2012, with another 150 yearly coming from other migrant destinations (chiefly Guam, the CNMI, and the United States), for a total of 450 new migrants a year.

At the time of the survey there were 1,985 Micronesian households in Hawaiʻi, with its total migrant population of 7,948. The average household contained four persons, and two of the four were earning an income (Hezel and Levin 2012, table H02). Hence, each earner supported an average of one additional person, for a dependency ratio of one to one. All the 1,985 migrant households except for 21 had some form of cash income. For those with some cash income, the average household income was $42,158, with half of the households receiving less than $34,804 each year (Hezel and Levin 2012, table H18).[15] The figures for median and mean household income in Hawaiʻi were much higher than the figures for Guam, despite the fact that the average Guam household was a third larger than that in Hawai'i.

The distinction between the relatively well-to-do FSM households and the poorer ones is striking. Of the 1,985 households, 38 percent were below poverty level on the index for Hawai'i (Hezel and Levin 2012, table HH18). Even so, it is encouraging to observe that the percentage of migrant households below the poverty level has fallen over the years, from 67 percent in 1997 to 45 percent in 2003 and 38 percent in 2012 (Levin 2003, table 4.14). The average income for these poorer households was just $13,929, far below the $42,000 average income of all FSM households in Hawai'i.

Thirty-five percent of all Micronesians aged 15 and over worked for cash, according to the survey (Hezel and Levin 2012, table H15). The jobs they held in Hawai'i were, for the most part, the typical entry-level positions that migrants might take anywhere—in fast-food places, small stores, and car washes; for delivery services; in hotels as housekeepers; or working as janitors, nursing aides, or night watchmen. The median salary was about $9 an hour—slightly higher than that earned among the migrants on Guam, but necessary to offset the higher cost of living in Hawai'i. As one person remarked in a focus-group discussion, unemployment is not a major problem for Micronesians "because most of the jobs that we are employed in are avoided by others." He went on to note, "If someone is unemployed, it is by choice."

Unemployment is not a major problem for Micronesians 'because most of the jobs that we are employed in are avoided by others.'

Not everyone was working at an entry-level position, however. Signs of job success in the migrant community were more striking in Hawai'i than in most other destinations. A handful of FSM people worked for the government, some as interpreters for the courts and others as teachers. One participant in the focus group pointed out that many Pohnpeians have found jobs in construction due to the fact that one or two of the early migrants were promoted to managerial positions in the construction companies. A handful of migrants have even become business owners. Another participant in the focus group pointed to Yapese as models in this respect. One Yapese runs a successful landscaping business on Hawai'i's Big Island. Another has founded a high-profile IT firm that has become a pioneer in the field. In addition, there are a few Micronesian doctors, including an eye doctor, and a number of military officers (although they had to become US citizens to obtain their commissions).

Homelessness has been a continuing problem for Micronesians in Hawai'i at least since FSM migration began to accelerate after 2000. In 2011, the year before the latest survey, over 1,200 FSM people took advantage of the Shelter Program for some period of time during the year. FSM people represented 15 percent of all those served by the shelters in the state.[16]

In recent years Micronesian migrants in Hawai'i have received bad press for criminal behavior, including a few well-publicized cases of homicide . Overall, there is a pattern of a growing number of arrests of FSM migrants, from an average of about 200 a year during the 1990s to 513 in 2003, 1,503 in 2006, and 2,717 in 2010 (the last year for which these data were available).[17] Of the 2,717 arrests made in 2010, however, all but 218 were for misdemeanors or less. During that same year, 180 FSM people were incarcerated for an average of 25 days each.[18]

US Mainland

The total Micronesian migrant population in the mainland United States was calculated at 24,048.[19] Migrants are distributed throughout almost the entire continental United States. Based on a list of thousands of migrants that was an outgrowth of the 2012 survey, we were able to piece together a listing of the main migrant sites in the United States along with a rough estimate of how large the FSM population is in each site.[20] The largest concentrations of FSM people seem to be in two places: Portland, Oregon, and the surrounding area and Kansas City, Missouri, and vicinity. Each of these sites is estimated to contain roughly 4,000 Micronesian migrants.

The other migrant sites, none of which approaches Portland or Kansas City in size, are too numerous to list here. Just as migrants have branched out from Portland to the Seattle area, the much smaller community in southern California has spread to Arizona and Nevada. There are a few hundred FSM people in Texas and Oklahoma, and a rapidly expanding migrant population in the Midwest—particularly in Wisconsin, Minnesota, and Iowa, and reaching over to Illinois and Ohio. Micronesians began spilling over into the Southeast, perhaps beginning in Florida in the late 1990s; now there are communities in Alabama, Georgia, the Carolinas, and Virginia. The northeastern states, with their larger population centers, have only been sparsely settled, but there are small groups of Micronesians in Pennsylvania, New York, Massachusetts, and Connecticut. Even Alaska has about a hundred Micronesians scattered in three different cities. Micronesians reside in at least 34 states today.

Migration to the mainland United States has accelerated during the past two decades. During the period from 1995 to 2000, the net gain of the migrant population there was 700 a year; over the following 12 years (2000–2012), the migrant population grew by 1,200 yearly (Hezel and Levin 2012, table M02).

The survey data show that for the five years preceding the survey, about 800 of these 1,200 were coming directly from the FSM, while another 400 were moving from other migrant destinations to settle in the US mainland (Hezel and Levin 2012, table M09). These data support the theory that step migration has become a common practice: Micronesians move to Hawai'i or Guam for a few years before they make the next move to the US mainland.

Step migration has become common: Micronesians move to Hawai'i or Guam for a few years before they make the next move to the US mainland.

Besides the yearly increase of 1,200 through migration itself, the 2012 survey recorded an average of 555 births to FSM migrants each year. Hence, the FSM population in the mainland United States was growing by a total of 1,755 yearly, although population loss through departures and deaths was not registered in this figure.

If FSM people migrate to the US mainland—as they do to other destinations—to find cash employment and provide for their families, the data gathered in the recent survey show that they are quite successful in achieving these aims. According to the survey, 63 percent (10,561) of Micronesians aged 15 years and older who migrated to the US mainland had paying jobs (Hezel and Levin 2012, table M12). This is a much higher percentage of wage earners than was found in any of the other destinations.

Many of the migrants, especially the new arrivals, held the same sorts of low-paying jobs that migrants to Guam and Hawai'i normally took. Micronesians interviewed in Portland mentioned work in the canneries, lumber yards, and airport concessions. They also spoke of sales in distribution warehouses, construction work in iron, and employment as cashiers or in housekeeping. One of the Kansas City groups highlighted employment in cheap restaurants, nursing homes, and plants that produce food. But there were also some well-paid educators and administrators, as well as those working for insurance companies and banks or doing translation for the government. One person from Yap was said to hold a very responsible position with a car rental agency that makes it necessary for him to travel widely throughout the country. Another, working in research and development, was often called on to represent his company in Paris and other international capitals.

As in other places, even those who begin at entry-level jobs sometimes advance up the employment ladder; some interviewees noted that several individuals who began as cashiers in fast-food places moved up to become managers. As one person observed, however, Micronesians tend to value job security more than opportunity for advancement. This, he explained, is the reason for the infrequent switchover from one job to another.

The median wage for migrants in the mainland United States was about $11 an hour, considerably higher than the hourly wage in Hawai'i and in Guam (Hezel and Levin 2012, table M15). For those who had regular wage employment, the median yearly salary was $19,448 and the average was $23,000 (Hezel and Levin 2012, table M18).

As we might expect, nearly all households (5,597 out of 5,954) had some cash income. The median household income was $46,594, while the average income was $62,844 (Hezel and Levin 2012, table M18). The relatively high household income of Micronesian migrants in the US mainland can be partially explained by the higher salaries there, but it is also due to the large percentage of migrants holding jobs and producing income in other ways. The 13,416 people who earned an income were distributed throughout 5,954 households (Hezel and Levin 2012, table M17). The survey data, therefore, indicated that each household (averaging 4 members) had 2.25 earners. In the mainland United States alone, of all the sites examined in the survey, there were more cash earners than dependents.

Although the survey data cannot be used to track homelessness, it is clear from discussions with FSM migrants that this is not a serious problem in the mainland United States. They attested that there is no homelessness at all in the towns or rural areas, and very little in the larger cities. One informed participant knew of eight young men from the FSM living on the street in the Portland area, but he added that their families would have gladly taken care of them. All heavy drinkers, they opted out of their households in favor of the freedom of life on the streets. As another person put it, those without homes are "homeless by choice" rather than by necessity, as is the case in Hawai'i and Guam.

Public housing assistance, so sought after in Guam and Hawai'i, was conspicuously absent in the mainland United States. Government subsidies toward private housing for low-income families—what is sometimes referred to as Section 8 benefits—are available only for US citizens in most states. Even if it were available, however, those Micronesians interviewed said that such assistance was not needed in any but a few cases.

Overview of Findings

The size of the Micronesian population living abroad, as counted in the 2012 survey, was 49,840. This total included those who moved from the FSM and children born to them in their new homes. Of the sites surveyed, the distribution of the FSM migrant population was as follows: Guam, 13,558; CNMI, 4,286; Hawai'i, 7,948; and the US mainland, 24,048.

Although no attempt was made in this survey to distinguish pre-Compact and post-Compact migrants, we can differentiate between those who left the FSM to live abroad and those who were born in the United States and its dependencies. Using the survey tables on birthplace as the norm, we find that 16,790 of the FSM population abroad were born on US soil: 5,544 were born on Guam, 2,350 in the CNMI, 1,903 in Hawai'i, and 6,993 in the US mainland. Thus, one-third of the total FSM population living abroad was born abroad.

The migrant population growth over the past five years (2007–2012) in each of the destinations can be determined from the survey data.[21]

- Guam has been getting 375 new Micronesian migrants a year—310 directly from the FSM (the great majority of them from Chuuk) and 65 from other places. Added to this are 355 births each year to FSM families. The FSM population on Guam is growing by 730 a year.
- CNMI has been receiving nearly 80 new migrants a year—62 directly from the FSM and 17 from other places. With 80 births yearly, the total FSM population increase comes to 160 a year.
- Hawai'i has registered 450 Micronesian migrants a year—300 directly from the FSM and 150 from elsewhere. With 140 new births yearly, there are 590 additions in all, minus the number of deaths and departures from the state.
- The US mainland has been getting 1,200 new migrants a year—800 directly from the FSM and 400 from other destinations such as Guam and Hawai'i. With 555 births to FSM families each year, the total yearly increase has been 1,755.

The total number of those truly migrating from the FSM (excluding children born overseas), as measured in the survey, is about 2,100 a year. Migration to the US mainland accounts for a little over half the migrant total. The data gathered in the survey also provide clear evidence of step-migration—that is, movement from an early destination (usually Guam or Hawai'i) to another one later (often mainland United States). There is also some evidence for back-migration, as when people who have ventured out later return home or to a closer destination.

Each year, new births increase the overseas FSM population by 1,130. Hence, one-third of the new FSM population abroad comes from births to

FSM migrants after they have settled in the United States and its territories.[22] On Guam, the number of births in recent years has been about the same as the number of new migrants, while in the CNMI the former is a little higher than the latter. In Hawai'i, the ratio of births to new migrants is roughly one to three, and in the US mainland it is about one to two.

Contrary to the belief that migrants usually live in overcrowded quarters, this survey found that the size of the migrant household was rather small compared with the average household in the FSM. The average number living in a housing unit on Guam was 5.4 persons, a drop from 7.2 just 20 years earlier. In the CNMI, the size was slightly smaller at 5.1. In both Hawai'i and the US mainland, the average size was 4.0 persons.

> **The size of the migrant household was rather small compared with the average household in the FSM.**

In the FSM, on the other hand, the average household size was 6.0 overall, ranging from 4.9 in Yap to 6.3 in Chuuk (FSM 2010, table H 2).

Even though the households were generally small, they showed considerable generational depth in the older and more established migrant communities of Guam and the CNMI. It was not unusual to find grandchildren living in the household, although the range of kinship among members of the household was probably not as broad as it might be in the FSM. The average household in Hawai'i and the US mainland, perhaps because it contained fewer people, did not show as much generational depth as the other two sites.

The survey showed that everyone who was not in school or taking care of the children seemed to be working. The number of earners—that is, those formally employed or bringing in money in some other way—was high relative to the number of those in the household. On Guam, there were 1.8 earners for the average household (5.6 persons). In the CNMI there were 1.4 earners per household (5.1 persons). In Hawai'i, there were 2 earners per household (4 persons), while in the mainland United States there were 2.2 earners for each household (4 persons). Another way of putting this is by calculating a support ratio: The average earner in the CNMI supported 2.6 others; on Guam, 2 others; in Hawai'i, 1 other; and in the mainland United States, 0.6 other people.[23] The percentage of workers per household increased, or the support ratio decreased, as FSM people moved farther away from their own islands. In the US mainland alone, of all the surveyed sites, there were more cash earners than non-earners among migrants.

The yearly income for the average household also increased as one moved eastward. The average household incomes, as recorded in the survey data, were as follows: CNMI, $25,450; Guam, $24,800; Hawai'i, $42,150; and the US mainland, $62,800. The difference becomes even greater when we show this as per capita income in each site: CNMI, $5,000; Guam, $4,600; Hawai'i, $10,500; and the US mainland, $15,700. While 74 percent of FSM households in the CNMI were living below the poverty line, the numbers dropped sharply in Hawai'i (38 percent) and the mainland United States (27 percent).

A surprising two-thirds (67 percent) of the FSM households in the mainland United States had health insurance (Hezel and Levin 2012, table MH10). This is in striking contrast with FSM communities in other locations, where it was rare for households to have health insurance. On Guam, only 13 percent were insured; in the CNMI, 16 percent; and in Hawai'i, 28 percent. The median premiums paid were $137 yearly. While the health insurance was rarely adequate to cover all medical expenses, migrants could call on their own churches and communities to help cover the remainder of their bills.

Reliance on welfare benefits declined notably as migrants moved farther away from home. On Guam, 58 percent of the households received food-stamp assistance; in the CNMI, 53 percent of the households were recipients; in Hawai'i, 46 percent; and in the mainland United States, 35 percent. The drop-off in numbers from west to east could reflect both the lower percentages of Micronesian children in Hawai'i and the US mainland and the relative prosperity of the FSM households in these sites. While 74 percent of FSM households in the CNMI were living below the poverty line, the numbers dropped sharply in Hawai'i (38 percent) and the mainland United States (27 percent). Other forms of welfare seem to have had minimal impact on FSM households. In Hawai'i, 31 percent of the households received supplemental welfare support, but in Guam only 10 percent did. In the CNMI (1.6 percent) and the US mainland (3 percent), welfare was negligible.

> **Reliance on welfare benefits declined notably as migrants moved farther away from home.**

Homelessness was a considerable problem on Guam (for about 650, or 5 percent of the migrant population) and in Hawai'i (for about 1,000, or 12 percent of migrants), but not in other places. In Guam and Hawai'i, homeless migrants from the FSM often sought help in public shelters. Elsewhere, the few instances of homelessness were self-chosen, as when an individual moved out to be free of the family, usually because of drinking or drug use.

The education background of the migrant populations revealed a significant change from what was found in past surveys. Although the migrant people aged 25 and older on Guam and in the CNMI still showed proportionately fewer bachelor's degrees than the resident population of the FSM, this was not the case in Hawai'i and mainland United States. Among the FSM migrants in Hawai'i, 5 percent held a bachelor's degree, while in the US mainland 6 percent had a full college degree—both higher than the 4.3 percent rate among the resident population in the FSM. The educational level of FSM people in both destinations, many of whom were recent arrivals, was higher than that in the FSM itself. Thus, the first signs of the long-anticipated brain drain have at last appeared.

FSM migrants may have left their home islands, but they clearly have not abandoned their kin ties, their culture, or their language. The survey data show that Micronesian migrants generally prefer to use their native language at home with their families, even if they must speak English most of the time in school or the workplace. FSM migrants everywhere, except for in the CNMI, claim to be in regular contact with their families back home through phone and the Internet. About one-third of the FSM migrants on Guam and in the US mainland had made at least one visit home, while almost half (46 percent) of the migrants in Hawai'i had been back.

> **The first signs of the long-anticipated brain drain have at last appeared.**

Remittances, the gifts of cash or material goods to assist family and friends back in the islands, are an important expression of migrants' continuing ties with home. In 2006, the value of remittances to FSM residents appeared to be close to $20 million a year.[24] It appeared that remittances might become a major source of income for the FSM, as it has long been for other island nations like Samoa, Tonga, Fiji, and the Cook Islands. But there are strong hints in the survey data that remittance patterns are changing. Migrants today seem to be sending home fewer clothes and other material goods, while cash remittance patterns may be shifting. Instead of sending money home at regular intervals, as many did some years ago, migrants seem to be sending cash in response to family needs—the purchase of a new car, a required church contribution, a birthday gift, or funeral expenses. Today, money is more frequently sent "on demand," at the request of the family back in the islands, rather than at the initiative of the migrant.

The total of remittance amounts recorded in the 2012 survey was surprisingly small, at $3 million. This is an amount far below what was expected and even less than the amount recorded as received by FSM households.[25] These data leave us a vital question touching on the future contribution of remittances to the FSM economy: Are remittances still a growing factor in the FSM, or has the age of remittances for the FSM ended almost as soon as it began?

Migration: A Fact of Life

Migration from the FSM has been a recent phenomenon, beginning in earnest some 25 years ago with the implementation of the Compact in 1986. Early migration routes were to Guam and the CNMI at first, then to Hawai'i, and finally to the US mainland. By 1995, there were well over 7,000 FSM citizens in the CNMI and Guam, with perhaps another 2,000 in Hawai'i and an equal number in the US mainland. In all, we can estimate that the total Micronesian migrant population at that time was about 12,000. This would indicate a yearly outflow of a little over 1,000 persons, or about 1 percent of the total population of the FSM. Chuukese came in greatest numbers during the earliest years (1986–1990), but soon afterward, the percentages of migrants from other states began to match that from Chuuk.

By 1995, the structural reforms underway in the FSM to prepare for the end of the first 15-year Compact-funding period were resulting in cuts in the number of government jobs throughout the nation. Since government had always been the bedrock of the island economy, the entire economy began to shrink. For the first time in over 40 years, there was no significant increase in the number of jobs. Thus began an employment plateau that has continued to the present.

With no new jobs to attract them at home, more Micronesians than ever began to seek their futures abroad. Most presumably left to find work, but others sought health care or education for their children. Consequently, the emigration rate doubled after the mid-1990s, so that just over 2 percent of the population, or over 2,000 persons a year, were leaving home to reside overseas during these years, as the intercensal population figures clearly suggest.[26] As far as we can tell, this same rate of migration has held up to the present day.

Although the migrant population on Guam had been growing steadily from 1997 and the number of Micronesians in Hawai'i had increased during the first decade of the new millennium, the favored destination during this time seems to have been the mainland United States. Half the new migrants were settling there, with over a thousand FSM citizens arriving each year.

Migration has become an inescapable fact in Micronesia in the past 25 years.

Migration has become an inescapable fact in Micronesia in the past 25 years. At present, nearly one-third of the total FSM-born population is living abroad. The emigration rate, which was roughly 1 percent of the population during the first few years of the Compact, has increased to 2 percent annually since the early 1990s. There is no sign that the yearly migration will be reduced any time soon. In fact, the chronic shortage of wage labor in the islands owing to a stagnant economy suggests quite the opposite. If the present rate of migration continues, we can expect that in another 20 years the FSM population abroad will be as large as the resident population in the islands. Even now, the Federated States of Micronesia has joined the cluster of Pacific Island nations—among them Tonga, Samoa, the Cook Islands, Niue, Kiribati, and Palau—that have seen a significant part of their population leave for destinations overseas.

Notes

---

[1] The emigration figures for Palau are derived from the "missing population" of the islands as computed from the difference between the actual resident population of Palau and the supposed population (computed by the addition of all recorded births less deaths in the preceding year). See Hezel and Levin 1990 for the figures.

[2] See especially Rubinstein 1990; Rubinstein 1993; Rubinstein and Levin 1992; Connell 1991; Smith 1994; Hezel and Levin 1996.

[3] In addition to this report by Smith based on interviews with Guamanian residents, another report made use of interviews with key FSM and Marshallese people. See Woo and Aguilar 1993.

[4] This was introduced as Bill No. 246 in the 23rd Guam Legislature in 1995.

[5] See, for instance, Will Hoover and Dan Nakaso, "Micronesians Fill the Homeless Shelters," *Honolulu Advertiser*, July 8, 2007.

[6] In an informal, unpublished survey of 51 migrant Micronesian families in Hawai'i and the mainland United States, conducted by Micronesian Seminar in 2006, the average household size was given as 4.2, with half the members of the household employed, on average.

[7] The figures drawn from the sample done by the US Census Bureau in 2008 were not used in the 2012 survey.

[8] The FSM resident population in 1994 was 105,506, according to a census done that year, while the resident population in 2010, another census year, was recorded as 102,843. The "missing population" for the 17-year period from 1995 through 2011, based on a 2.1 percent natural growth rate per year, would come to 40,300. Adding this to 9,700—the number of FSM residents who migrated prior to 1994—yields an estimated total Micronesian migrant population of about 50,000.

[9] The population projection found in this report by the government of Guam is based on the assumed growth rate between 2003 and 2008, using the US Census Bureau figures for the latter year and an extension of this same growth rate to the present.

[10] The 2003 figure is found in Levin 2003, table 4.1, while the figure for the FSM resident population is from the unpublished data from FSM 2010, table B-1.

[11] The 1992 figure was taken from University of Guam and GovGuam 1993, table 31. The figures for 1997 and 2003 can be found in Levin 2003, table 4.8.

[12] The figures for homelessness were provided by the Guam Homeless Coalition, which does a periodic Point-in-Time Homeless Count. The more recent figure was for January 2012.

[13] The total number of arrests for that year (2,682) is recorded in Guam Police Department 2010, table 4.1. The arrests of FSM people (1,689) for the same year is taken from a report sent from the Guam Police Department to the Guam Bureau of Statistics and Plans for use in the Compact-impact report for that year.

[14] The total number of arrests for each of these years is found in the Uniform Crime Report, produced annually by the Guam Police Department, while the number of FSM people arrested each year is listed in the yearly reports supplied by the Police Department to the Guam Bureau of Statistics.

[15] The average income of the Micronesian household in Hawai'i has risen over the years: it was $9,000 in 1996, $21,000 in 2003, and $42,000 in 2012. These figures are not adjusted for inflation, however. See Brekke, Filibert, and Hammond 2008; 32.

[16] Officials in the shelter program were quick to point out that this figure (1,253) does not count those housed in shelters at a given time; rather, it reflects the number of applications for assistance from FSM people during the year. In some cases, the same person might apply for housing assistance more than once. Hence, the figure for Micronesians in shelters is lower than this number.

[17] The figures on arrests are found in the following State of Hawai'i Compact of Free Association (COFA) impact reports: 2002, exhibit D; 2007, exhibits F and I; and 2011, exhibit H.

[18] See State of Hawai'i COFA impact report for 2011, exhibits H and I.

[19] The method was simply to subtract the total FSM migrant population in the other destinations (Guam, CNMI, and Hawai'i) from the total estimated migrant population from the FSM to determine the base number of FSM people in the US mainland. The means used to calculate the total FSM migrant population since 1986 is explained above in note 8.

[20] This list is not part of this report inasmuch as it is unsupported by the survey data, but the list can be made available upon request.

[21] The figures below have been rounded off from the data in the tables.

[22] This means, of course, that the overall increase in the FSM migrant population, including births abroad, would come to 3,200 a year. This is not at all an unrealistic figure, especially since the data being examined here do not take into account migrant population loss through death and departure.

[23] Here, this ratio is used rather than the standard dependency ratio so as to avoid having to introduce ages into the calculation.

[24] This figure was based on the remittances recorded in a convenience sample of migrants. The total extrapolated remittance figure for the FSM was then checked for congruence against data from money-transfer agencies operating in the FSM.

[25] There is a large disparity between the remittance data in this survey and data collected in the FSM. The 2010 FSM Census (table B-19) records the total yearly remittance value as $14,144,000, with the average household in the FSM receiving $2,553.

[26] The resident population of the FSM, according to census figures, was 105,500 in 1994, 107,200 in 2000, and 102,600 in 2010.

References

Brekke, Eunice, Canisius Filibert, and Ormond Hammond. 2008. *A Study of Individuals and Families in Hawai'i From the Federated States of Micronesia, the Republic of the Marshall Islands, and Other Northern Pacific Islands.* Honolulu: Pacific Resources for Education and Learning.

CNMI. *See* Commonwealth of the Northern Mariana Islands.

Commonwealth of the Northern Mariana Islands. 1994. *Survey of Micronesians in the CNMI.* Saipan: CNMI, Central Statistics Division.

_____. 2000. *Impact of the Compacts of FAS Citizens on the CNMI for Fiscal Year 1999.* Saipan: CNMI, Governor's Office.

Connell, John. 1991. "The New Micronesia: Pitfalls and Problems of Dependent Development." *Pacific Studies* 14 (2), 87–120.

Connell, John and Richard P.C. Brown. *2005 Remittances in the Pacific: An Overview.* Manila: Asian Development Bank. March 2005.

Coulter, Paulette M. 1993. *Impacts of Migration from the Compact of Free Association States on Public and Selected Private Agencies on Guam.* Mangilao, Guam: University of Guam, Micronesian Language Institute.

Federated States of Micronesia. 1982. *Compact of Free Association and Related Agreements Between the Federated States of Micronesia and the United States of America.* Pohnpei: Federated States of Micronesia.

_____. 1994. *Census of Population and Housing, Preliminary Counts.* Pohnpei: Federated States of Micronesia, Office of Planning and Statistics.

_____. 2010. *Census of Population and Housing.* Unpublished tables. Pohnpei: Federated States of Micronesia, Office of Planning and Statistics.

FSM. *See* Federated States of Micronesia.

GAO. *See* US Government Accountability Office.

Government of Guam. 1996. *Pacific Immigration Impact: Effects of PL 99–239 on the Island of Guam, FY 1989 to FY 1995.* Hagatna, Guam: Government of Guam, Office of the Governor.

_____. 2000. *Impact of Compacts of Free Association, FY 1996-FY 2000.* Hagatna, Guam: Government of Guam, Office of the Governor.

_____. 2004. *Compact Impact Reconciliation: Guam's Unreimbursed Costs of the Compacts of Free Association, Fiscal Year 1987 to Fiscal Year 2003.* Hagatna, Guam: Government of Guam, Office of the Governor.

_____. 2011. *Impact of the Compacts of Free Association on Guam, FY 2004–2011.* Hagatna, Guam: Government of Guam, Office of the Governor.

GovGuam. *See* Government of Guam.

Guam Police Department. 2010. *Crime in Guam,* 2010. *Uniform Crime Reports.* Hagatna, Guam: Guam Police Department.

Hezel, Francis X. 1979. "The Education Explosion in Truk." *Pacific Studies* 2.2 (Spring), 167–85.

Hezel, Francis X, and Michael J. Levin. 1990. "Micronesian Emigration: The Brain Drain in Palau, Marshalls and the Federated States." In *Migration and Development in the South Pacific,* ed. John Connell, 42–60. Canberra: Australian National University.

_____. 1996. "New Trends in Micronesian Migration." *Pacific Studies* 19.1 (March), 91–114.

_____. 2012. *Survey of Federated States of Micronesia Migrants in the United States including Guam and the Commonwealth of Northern Mariana Islands (CNMI).* Report presented to the FSM national government, Pohnpei.

Hezel, Francis X., and Thomas B. McGrath. 1989. "The Great Flight Northward: FSM Migration to Guam." *Pacific Studies* 13.1 (November), 47–64.

Hezel, Francis X., and Eugenia Samuel. 2006. "Micronesians Abroad." *Micronesian Counselor* 64.

Levin, Michael J. 1997. *Micronesian Migrants to Guam, Hawai'i and the Commonwealth of the Northern Mariana Islands: A Study of the Impact of the Compacts of Free Association.* Washington, DC: US Bureau of the Census.

_____. 1998. *The Impact of the Compacts of Free Association on the United States Territories and Commonwealths and on the State of Hawai'i.* Washington: US Department of the Interior, Office of Insular Affairs.

_____. 2003. *The Status of Micronesian Migrants in the Early 21st Century: A Second Study of the Impact of the Compacts of Free Association Based on Censuses of Micronesian Migrants to Hawai'i, Guam, and the Commonwealth of the Northern Mariana Islands.* Cambridge, Massachusetts: Harvard University, Population and Development Studies Center.

Roche, Walter F., and Mariano Willoughby. 2002. "Ruthless Trade of the 'Body-Builders.'" *Baltimore Sun,* September 16.

Rubinstein, Donald H. 1990. "Coming to America: Micronesian Newcomers in Guam." Paper presented at the College of Arts and Sciences Research Conference, University of Guam, March 5.

_____. 1993. "Movements in Micronesia: Post-Compact (1987) Micronesian Migrants to Guam and Saipan." In *A World Perspective on Pacific Islander Migration, Australia, New Zealand and the USA*, ed. Grant McCall and John Connell. Kensington, NSW: University of New South Wales, Centre for South Pacific Studies.

Rubinstein, Donald H., and Michael J. Levin. 1992. "Micronesian Migration to Guam: Social and Economic Characteristics." *Asian and Pacific Migration Journal* 1 (2), 350–385.

Smith, Sedya Turk. 1993. *Attitudes of Long-Term Residents of Guam Toward the Immigrants from the Federated States of Micronesia and the Republic of the Marshall Islands.* Mangilao, Guam: University of Guam, Micronesian Language Institute.

Ullman, Michael D. 2007. *The Not-So-Silent Epidemic, The Rise in Shelter Utilization by Micronesians in Hawai'i, 2001 to 2006.* Unpublished.

US Census Bureau. 1980. *Guam Census.* PC 80-a-c D54. Washington, DC: US Department of Commerce.

_____. 1990. *US Census of Population and Housing: Social, Economic and Housing Characteristics: Guam.* Washington, DC: US Department of Commerce.

_____. 2000. *US Census of Population and Housing: Social, Economic and Housing Characteristics: Guam.* Washington, DC: US Department of Commerce.

_____. 2009. *Final Report: 2008 Survey of Compact of Free Association (COFA) Migrants.* Washington, DC: US Department of Commerce.

US Government Accountability Office. 2011. *Compacts of Free Association: Improvements Needed to Assess and Address Growing Migration.* GAO-12-64. Washington, DC: US Government Accountability Office.

Woo, Ginlin, and Viviana Aguilar. 1993. *The Impact of the Compact Migration for the Federated States of Micronesia and the Republic of the Marshall Islands: A Summary of Interviews with Key Representatives from the Compact Freely Associated States.* Mangilao, Guam: University of Guam, Micronesian Language Institute.

The Author

Francis X. Hezel, SJ, has lived and worked in Micronesia for over four decades. Originally from Buffalo, New York, he first arrived in the islands in 1963 as a classroom teacher at Xavier High School in what was then Truk District, the US Trust Territory of the Pacific Islands. In 1969, he was ordained a priest in the Jesuit order, returned to the islands, and soon became director of Xavier High School. In 1972 he was named director of Micronesian Seminar, the church-based, research-pastoral institute established to engage in public education throughout the Micronesian region. He served in this position for 38 years until his replacement in 2010.

During his years with Micronesian Seminar, Hezel organized dozens of conferences on a variety of public issues and gave personal presentations at dozens of other conferences. He produced over 70 video documentaries for local broadcast, including a seven-hour series on the history of Micronesia. He also introduced a popular website that offers Micronesians everywhere the opportunity to access Micronesian Seminar products and to discuss contemporary issues with one another.

A self-taught historian, Hezel's influence on Micronesian studies has been described as formidable. He is the author of 10 books on Micronesia, including *Making Sense of Micronesia: The Logic of Pacific Island Culture* (University of Hawai'i Press, 2013), and more than 100 other publications, including articles, monographs, and textbooks. Hezel is frequently consulted within and beyond Micronesia by government officials, educators, researchers, and development specialists. He has received honorary doctorate degrees from the University of Guam and Fordham University, his alma mater. Most recently, Hezel has been preparing follow-up projects related to Micronesian migrants abroad, in collaboration with the Micronesian government.

Submissions

Submissions to Pacific Islands Policy may take the form of a proposal or completed manuscript (ideally, 7,000–11,000 words), and should be accompanied by a curriculum vitae indicating the author's relevant credentials and publications. Proposals should indicate the issue to be analyzed, its policy significance, the contribution the analysis will provide, and the date by which the manuscript will be ready. The series editors and editorial board will review proposals and manuscripts. If a manuscript is considered suitable for the series, it will be peer-reviewed. Submissions must be original and not published elsewhere. Authors will be asked to assign copyright to the East-West Center.

Notes to Contributors

Manuscripts should be prepared in Microsoft Word, double-spaced, and submitted via email. The preferred documentation style is for citations to appear in the text (*The Chicago Manual of Style* author-date system) and accompanied by a complete reference list. Notes should be electronically embedded in the Word file. All artwork should be camera ready. Send submissions and queries to the series editors:

Gerard A. Finin
Resident Codirector
FininG@EastWestCenter.org

Robert C. Kiste
Adjunct Senior Fellow
KisteR@EastWestCenter.org

Pacific Islands Development Program
East-West Center
1601 East-West Road
Honolulu, Hawai'i 96848 USA

Tel: 808.944.7745
Fax: 808.944.7670
EastWestCenter.org/PacificIslandsPolicy

www.ingramcontent.com/pod-product-compliance
Lightning Source LLC
Chambersburg PA
CBHW060523280326
41933CB00014B/3083